Got Dogs?

What To Do With Fido When You Travel

Easy tips to help you determine if you should bring Fido on your trip; leave him home with a pet sitter; or take him to a pet hotel, dog ranch, dog boarding kennel or your trusted veterinarian.

By, Cindy J. Hill

Your Pet Advocate

"Helping you choose the best animal care for your family"

Published by CinCO Enterprises Inc.

Copyright © 2011 CinCO Enterprises Inc.

2nd addition May 2012

Printed in the United States of America

Hill, Cindy J.;

Got Dogs? What To Do With Fido When You Travel / Easy tips to help you determine if you should bring Fido on your trip; leave him home with a pet sitter; or take him to a pet hotel, dog ranch, dog boarding kennel or your trusted veterinarian.; by Cindy J. Hill

ISBN-13: 978-0615493497 (CinCO Enterprises Inc,)

ISBN-10: 0615493491

To order please visit www.GotDogsBooks.com

For more information visit www.YourPetAdvocate.com

Cover Design by Dawn Teagarden

Photographs by Cindy J. Hill

This book is dedicated to my husband Brad;
our canine family members Sierra, Weya and Zahra
and all the dogs who have stayed at our dog ranch:
Mystic Mountain Pet Retreat.

I thank all the dogs in the world for their
patience, guidance and continued education
of how dogs see the world.

Table of Contents

Introduction 6

About The Author 8

Chapter 1: Review Fido's Personality,
Health and Energy 13

Chapter 2: Review Yourself,
What Is Your Desire For You and Fido? 27

Chapter 3: Dog Care Option #1 -
Bring Fido With You 33

Chapter 4: Dog Care Option #2 -
Leave Fido At Home, With a Friend or a Pet Sitter................. 43

Chapter 5: Dog Care Option #3 -
Take Fido To a Professional Pet Hotel, Dog Ranch,
Dog Boarding Kennel or Pet Care Center 57

Chapter 6: Getting Ready For Your Trip -
Dropping Off and Picking Up Fido 93

Chapter 7: Final Thoughts 102

Introduction

Got dogs and heading out of town for vacation, work or family? Ensuring quality care for Fido when you are away from home is part of being a good dog parent and having backup care for emergencies should be part of every family's plan.

In the past most people had family or neighbors check in on the family dog or they took Fido with them. Due to busy lives, having dogs that require extra care or just wanting Fido to benefit from more activity and attention the modern family needs more choices for their furry family member when they travel.

Even if you currently have care for Fido that you trust, having the knowledge about all the various pet care choices will help you if your current caregivers are unavailable or if your dog changes over time.

In the following pages we will review Fido's individual personality including age, health, exercise and emotional needs. We will also go over the owner's character, finances and wishes before moving on to the next step to help ensure your choice matches both you and Fido.

Once you know your own and Fido's desires then we go over all the possible dog care choices. From bringing him with you, to having your family care for Fido or using professional care including dog ranches, pet resorts, commercial boarding kennels, vets, day care centers or home pet care with a pet sitter you will have peace of mind knowing Fido is well cared for while you travel.

Even though the author owns and operates a custom dog care ranch her intent is not to promote one style of care; she knows that each dog's care must match the dog and family. All choices have pros and cons that the owner must consider for their own dog and family.

Finally with steps on how to get ready for your trip and free checklists no matter what your care choice is, you will come home to a healthy and happy dog.

Fido will love you!

For more information see: www.YourPetAdvocate.com
"Helping you choose the best animal care for your family"

About The Author

Cindy Hill lives on a 5 acre ranch near the foothills of the Cascade Range outside of Seattle with her husband Brad. They share their home with Weya and Zahra the active Ridgebacks, Sierra the security guard Cattle Dog; Jasper, Topaz and Onyx the kitties; Britches and Chenoa, Cindy's equine partners; Colton and Quincy the llama friends; Peach and Tina the crazy ferrets; Luna the sweet rabbit; six doves to provide soothing background music; and thirteen free range chickens for bug control and fresh eggs.

Cindy's past dogs included: Jasmine, the sweet Golden who developed a third degree heart block at the age of 2 which required a pacemaker; Rhombus, the shepherd/ husky mix and Olaf, the hound/lab whom both loved horse riding and running in the woods and developed serious arthritis in their later years they lived to a distinguished 14 and 15 years; Zimbabwe, the handsome rescue Ridgeback while loving and active had emotional issues from his past family and required delicate handling; Herman, the crazy Cattle dog who adopted us while on a walk in the woods would chase anything and loved to manage the family, developed malignant melanoma cancer and passed after a 2 and half year battle at the age of 14.

Cindy's quest for dog knowledge developed over the years due to having dogs and other animals with many diverse special needs. Rhombus caused her to find alternative veterinary, acupuncture and nutrition care; Olaf sent her to energy healing and warm water spa treatments; Herman showed her that chiropractic, homeopathic, nutrition and conventional treatments work well together; and her new Ridgebacks show how starting with a puppy from a holistic and caring small breeder can help create a balanced and healthy dog. Olaf, Herman, Sierra and Zimbabwe helped her develop the skills required when adopting rescues with various emotional upbringings.

During the 80's and 90's Cindy and Brad's vacations were mostly camping trips in the Pacific Northwest so brining the dogs along was fun for all. For the few trips that the dogs could not join the journey, they relied on friends and family or one of them stayed home to care for everyone.

The year of 2000 the family included newly adopted 100lb "Zimbabwe" who had past issues with children, crazy Cattle Dog "Herman" who liked to police everyone, and 13 year 60lb "Olaf" who had lost the use of his hind legs due to the arthritis along his whole spine.

Having three special needs dogs at one time required many changes to daily life. At first the solution was that Cindy and Brad did not travel together to support the care of the family. That changed when Brad's sister was to be married in Alaska so both needed to attend.

Before this time Cindy had never considered using a boarding facility but there was no way they could leave Zimbabwe, Herman and Olaf with un-trained people so family and friends were not an option. As Olaf was just starting to get feeling back in his legs Cindy was referred by her holistic vet to La Paw Spa for water therapy and found they also had a custom boarding ranch, an answer to their prayers for the wedding trip.

The ranch was able to care for the varied dogs requirements including giving Olaf's many supplements with a special diet and caring for the more active but emotionally unstable younger dogs.

Learning about the ranch opened up a whole new world of possibilities for Cindy who at the time was planning on opening an animal sanctuary when she retired from corporate life. Cindy then determined that she could not wait an additional 15 years to work with animals' full time and that 25 years at Microsoft and Boeing as a Project Manager was enough years working away from animals.

After much soul searching Cindy decided that she could still follow her core vision with a custom boarding service that catered to special needs animals and their humans and with her business skills opened her own pet care retreat and dog ranch www.MysticMountainRetreat.Com.

From caring for the numerous diverse dog guests since 2005 and discussing their varied situations and needs with their Moms and Dads; the idea for this book started developing. Even though Cindy owns Mystic Mountain Pet Retreat she knows that one solution will not be a fit for every dog at every stage of their life. Cindy wanted to provide an outline of the many options so people could determine the best choice for them, their family and their dog when they traveled.

Cindy's goal is that you enjoy this book and that it helps you to have relaxed and pleasurable trips knowing that Fido is well cared for.

For more information, articles, blogs, forms and checklists please see www.YourPetAdvocate.com.

Woof Woof,

Cindy Hill, Your Pet Advocate

"Helping you choose the best animal care for your family"

"All Creatures Great and Small"

Chapter 1
Review Fido's Personality, Health and Energy

The first step in deciding on the best care for your dog is to review his individuality, health and emotional background before choosing who will care for him when you travel or are busy. As dogs come in many different body suits with vast variables in physical, mental and health traits you will need to reflect about your dog's specific needs.

Different individualities to consider:

- Size: Giant, large, medium, small, very small

- Coat: Short, long, kinky fur

- Breed: Poodle, lab, bully, terrier, toy

- Temperament: active, laid back, wants to be held, needs a job, happy just hanging, loves to play with the gang

- Socialization: hates or fears other dogs; dominant, social, timid; fearful, bold, happy-go-lucky; likes everyone, wary of others, tend to only like some friends

- Health: special needs, arthritis, allergies, disabled, cancer, diabetes, epilepsy, deaf, blind, healthy

- Age: puppy, youth, adult, geriatric

- Status: neutered, spayed, intact (not fixed)

- Diet & Veterinarian Care: dry food, canned, raw food, homemade food. Requires medication or other supplements, follows holistic health care programs or other special needs.

You get the picture there are several variables that determine the best care option from types, personalities and varied health or age. It's up to you to figure out Fido's personality and needs then match him to the many different dog care choices when you travel or are busy.

Caring for the many different sizes, shapes, energy and health of dogs at Mystic Mountain Pet Retreat has taught me much over the years and here are a few examples from our guests:

"When Molly and Max, two lab mixes first started coming to camp they were only 6 months old and they enjoyed playing with the large community play group of about 10 dogs. Over the years Molly started getting ball possessive so we started having Molly play one on one with Max and the Caregivers; Max still got to go out with the big community group as he enjoyed it and did well with the other guests."

"Robby, a large Irish Wolfhound, is still intact but has wonderful social skills. He loves to play with the other guests and we make sure he is not mixed with other unneutered males or females."

"Dixie and Sage, two smaller rescue dogs with major separation anxiety including uncontrolled barking and spasms needed care for an upcoming trip. After an initial discussion their mom, Cathy determined that having an in-home professional stay with her pups was the best choice at that time. If Cathy wanted to have them stay overnight away from the home she would need to start training them to be calm and balanced at home, even starting with a few hours and working up to an overnight then an weekend trip before heading away for a longer trip."

"*Rufus, a very happy Goldendoodle who loves playing with other guests, has major motion sickness. Even after working with a holistic vet, drives that are more than a few miles are traumatic. Luckily, he lives just down the road so staying at the retreat works well. If there was not a good dog facility nearby, then having in-home care would be the best choice for Rufus.*"

"*Bella, a poodle, was a regular at the ranch until her dad got divorced and started traveling 20 out of 30 days. Her dad found another home to share her with, this was much better for Bella and much cheaper for her dad and the part time home got a pup without the full time care and money commitment.*"

The huge lesson that I have learned is that there is no "one" care style that fits all dogs all the time over their entire life.

Each person must determine the right choice for their own dog and family.

Fido May Enjoy Their Own Vacation

Consider that many dogs love new experiences that are different than their day to day schedule. Once used to the new surroundings, Fido may enjoy his own vacation away from his daily responsibilities of caring for the human family and property.

Some may feel that their dog is too shy or timid to be away from home, but a dog ranch or other care facility can help build confidence in stressed or nervous dogs. You will need to determine if a vacation away from home is the right choice for your pup.

> **"With the right environment dogs love new experiences."**

Dogs Love to be Dogs and it's Healthy for Dogs to be Dogs

Dogs play games with each other in different ways than they play with us humans, so having Fido play with other dogs develops healthy mind and body. If your dog goes to dog parks or plays with other dogs, think about finding a dog camp or place where your dog will get group play.

If your dog is timid or insecure and could use more time around other dogs consider a place that will allow your dog to play but ensures that all interactions are healthy for mind and spirit. Also some individual training to build their confidence is helpful.

Remember that dogs will change over time; just because they do well in an all free range or group/community play environment now does not mean they will always enjoy it. Confirm that the caregivers can separate the dogs if needed due to aging, mental or other health issues.

Some Dogs May Like Staying Home

Staying home with all the comforts and familiarity of the family setting may be the right choice for some dogs. Older or shy dogs may do better in their own environment. Ensure that Fido will get enough human interaction and outside activity even if he sleeps a lot or has low activity. For active dogs make sure they get enough walks and other mental activities.

Having Fido staying at home may cause him to wonder when you are coming home and how you are doing. When dogs are at another location and having fun with their dog friends they are in a different world. This may cause them to think and worry less about their humans or normal responsibilities, allowing them to be free to have fun. This is even more important to think about for longer trips.

In-home care may be a great choice for shorter trips; for longer trips, Fido may benefit from other choices. What would Fido do best with?

Small Dogs

If Fido is small and gets scared easily find a caregiver that provides small and monitored play groups to ensure all dog interactions are positive or that they will play with them separately. Make certain that toy dogs will get plenty of human holding and affection.

Some small active dogs, like terriers, may enjoy playing with the bigger active dogs while small shyer dogs may do well mixed with larger dogs only if they are older and or very mellow.

Rescued Dogs

Many dogs that have been rescued from a shelter worry about being left again; so make sure your choice works with them to build up their confidence. Some do better staying at home while others do better at a dog camp. If you are planning a long trip away from home, help Fido out by taking a few shorter trips so he can get used to your travel and new caregivers.

If your choice of care facility has doggie play sessions, make sure the caregiver provides groups that are small and monitored to ensure all dog interactions are positive or that the humans will play with them separately if needed.

For the stressed dog consider Thunder Jacket's or wraps that add overall pressure to the body of the dog which is reported to reduce stress. Also TTouch therapy or massage helps greatly with anxiety, either with a professional or you can learn the techniques from books or classes.

Energetic Dogs

If Fido is a hunting or active dog then ensuring that he gets plenty of activity is a must. Only consider home care if his energy needs can be met. Lots of play, walks and training should be part of his daily schedule. Active dogs will go crazy staying in crates or kennels all day with only potty breaks; dog camps are a great choice for the active dog.

Puppies Need Extra Care

Puppies should be considered special needs as they may require extra training, extra feeding, may not be potty trained and any emotional stresses can have lifetime impacts.

Having your young dog go to a facility with group interactions may help with his early socialization. Find care that can provide the special attention needed to ensure all interactions are healthy with the other dogs and their new environment.

Discuss with your vet what shots are needed and when for the type of care facility you are thinking of. Safety should be first for your new puppy.

Older Dogs or Health Issues Require Extra Care

Finding a special care provider for an older dog or one with health issues will involve more research than for young and healthy dogs. Having Fido stay at home should only be used if the caregiver has the knowledge and time to care for your dog's special needs.

Considerations:

- Special food, supplements, medications administration.

- Limited physical ability including eyes, hearing or walking; watch out for slick floors and steps.

- Extra emotional support.

- Ensuring other dogs won't jump up on an older dog's back or scare them.

- Limited bathroom ability.

- Massage, Reiki, swimming, other therapies that may help Fido during your trip.

If Fido Should Not Play With Other Dogs

Some dogs should not be mixed with other dogs for many reasons; this does not mean they have to stay alone at home or stay in a traditional kennel with nothing to do. Ensure that your caregiver provides safe interactive care, either at home or at custom dog facilities.

As with any special needs care, finding the best match will just take time. Determine the reasons why your dog should not be mixed. This could be due to aggression, dominance, being timid, if they are intact or other health reasons.

Dogs with behavioral issues could benefit with extra training to help them interact with other dogs. Ensure the caregivers know how to evaluate your dog and who if any other dogs that they can be mixed with.

If your dog is intact (not fixed) that does not mean they can't be mixed or play with other dogs, they may require extra supervision and matching of dogs. Some places won't accept your dog but many boarding kennels will evaluate your dog based on his behavior not his status.

If your dog is aggressive around other dogs or people; confirm "everyone" who will be around your dog is trained to ensure the safety of all involved. Provide all history of past aggressions and possible triggers. If you can't guarantee the caregivers knowledge then find other care or consider skipping your trip.

Holistic Health and Feeding Programs

Following a holistic, custom feeding or limited vaccination program will also determine your dog care choices. Do not worry there are places and people who can care for Fido, it just takes more effort to find them.

Many veterinarians are now recommending reduced vaccination programs. While many kennels still require numerous yearly shots, there are some smaller boarding places or dog ranches that will work with you and your veterinarian's recommendations.

Feeding your dog custom foods; be they homemade, raw, or a combination of dry and special canned and supplements, will require finding someone that understands the storage and handling of these foods.

"Put yourself into your dog's fur,
where would you like to be
if you were Fido and
had time on your Paws?"

Is Fido a Security Risk?

For active, insecure, or escape artist dogs think about their physical security when determining your dog's care. When you travel, Fido may try to find you.

Many homes and yards are not designed with dog security in mind. If Fido is a high security risk, a professional facility where they have experience preventing escapes may be the best choice. If you choose to have home-care make sure they know if Fido is a door darter, a fence climber or a digger. Also make sure Fido has extra dog tags with friends phone numbers in case of escape, this is in addition to chipping.

Dogs Are Social Animals and Can Get Bored Left Alone

Being bored for long periods either at home or in a traditional kennel may cause stress and separation anxiety. Dogs are social animals and most like to be around other dogs and or people, determine your dog's individual needs.

Many pet sitters come to the home for 20 – 30 minutes two or three times a day, is this enough for your dog?

If Fido is staying at home consider adding extra walks or have trainers come to the home. If your trip is longer than a few days an interactive dog camp may be a good choice for him.

Consider Training For Fido While You Travel

Additional learning helps the mind and body; consider training for Fido while you travel. Look for places that provide structured and challenging exercise to train them fully and help them to be happy dogs. If Fido is staying at home you can have a trainer visit them.

- Learning to be calm and centered in training helps develop the brain to be calm in other situations according to Temple Grandin doctor of animal science and behavior.

- One-on-one training gives Fido individual attention that he may not get during group play.

- Some places offer "unusual" or "experience" instruction like herding, being around farm animals, walks to city parks, hikes in the woods, agility or even trips into town.

- Ensure your trainer's methods match your dog and your own beliefs; ask what type of training they have, what techniques and tools they utilize.

"Will knowing that your dog is playing
and having fun at camp or resting
at home help you to have a clear mind
to have fun and relax yourself?"

"Choosing the right dog care is important to
ensure peace of mind while you travel."

Chapter 2

Review Yourself, What Is Your Desire For You and Fido?

Review your own character traits and desires before deciding who will care for Fido when you travel. If knowing that your dog is having his needs met, is safe and happy will you have a better vacation? Yes!

Think about your past trips. Were you uneasy about Fido being scared, bored or if he was eating? Will knowing that your dog is playing and having fun at camp or resting at home make your heart glow and help you to have a clear mind to have fun and relax yourself? Choosing the right care is important to ensure peace of mind while you travel.

"A happy dog equals a happy human"

In the past we have had many different types of care for our pets while we vacationed. Our choices depended on how long we were gone, if they had any special needs care and how available our friends, family and neighbors were.

There were times when having someone stay in the house worked well, while other trips we just did not want anyone staying in our home. For some trips getting the house ready was more work than taking the pups to a dog camp, other times I did not feel our fencing was adequate while we were away or that our dogs needed special care that a professional could provide.

One of the most stressful parts of traveling for people with pets is how Fido and Kitty are doing; I was no different than most. Even when I left the crew at home with my husband I would worry if all was well. While it may be impossible to not worry about your dog the more you plan, research and determine the best care for Fido the more you can enjoy and focus on your trip.

Once we started caring for dogs at our ranch I have heard many stories about the various types of care and how important it is that it matches the owner as well as the dog. People come in as many different personalities and needs as their dog friends and there is no one solution for all.

'Pam was a worrier about her Terrier Bella. Was she getting enough attention, eating enough and taking all her supplements?'

'The parents of Kali, a 3 legged Rotty who lived in a condo near Pike Place Market, enjoyed knowing she was running around on grass and being in the country.'

'The biggest concern for Morgan's Dad was special handling and training as Morgan was a newly rescued German Shepherd with fear aggression towards other dogs.'

'Nigel's Mom needed to know that her crazy bull dog who had seizures was in a safe physical space getting his medication 3 times a day and getting love and exercise.'

Concerns About Special Diets, Medication, Health, Physical and Emotional Needs

Are you are a worrier about your dog when you travel and have concerns about special diets, medication, health and emotional needs? Will spending extra money on custom care help your trip be more relaxed?

Doing research to confirm that the caregiver has the necessary knowledge to care for each dog's individual needs is important.

Some people feel better knowing Fido is at home. Others feel better if Fido is at a dog camp playing or around family and if your dog has medical needs staying at the vet may be best. So again, every owner needs to look within and trust their own feelings.

In-Home Care Considerations

An in-home caregiver can make your home look lived in and they can perform other tasks including turning on and off lights, watering plants, bringing in mail, and caring for other animals. Also, having a car drive in and out can be great; however if the caregiver is an professional, check to see if there are logos on the car. This may alert strangers or even neighbors that you are not home.

Some individuals do not like having people in their home when they are not there. So if you are considering in-home care, think about that. Will having caregivers in your home make you nervous or does it make you feel better?

Where do You Live? Do You Have a Car?

- If you are able and willing to drive then your choices of care are much greater.

- Many dog ranches or custom care facilities are outside of the city and can be more than an hour away.

- Dog taxi services may help get Fido to Camp but still do your research and visit the facility before your trip to ensure it's a great place and so your dog can smell the place before his stay.

Limited Money Creates Creative Options

If money is a concern you may have limited options in pet care; with effort, you can still find quality care for Fido.

- Check with your local veterinarian; many veterinarian techs are looking for extra income at a lower price than professional care.

- Neighbor kids are always a possible choice; confirm they are responsible and the level of care your dog needs matches the kid's ability and that you have an adult as a backup.

- Neighborhood seniors who love dogs may be a great choice; see about trading services for dog care like driving to doctors' visits, home repairs, gardening, or providing dinners.

- Try dog sharing if you travel often; some people would love to care for a dog but do not have time and money for a full time pup.

- Join a group that helps you connect with other pet owners for pet sharing, check out "PetWatchClub" or search on "pet exchange" or "pet sharing". As with any person caring for your dog ask questions and only trust someone who has the background to care for your dog and his needs.

Chapter 3
Dog Care Option #1
Bring Fido With You

Traveling with dogs can be lots of fun, but make certain this is the right choice for Fido, for you and for the specific trip planned.

Do you have experience traveling with dogs? How are you traveling? Car, flying, other? Again ask yourself if traveling with a dog is the best choice for you and for Fido before heading out. Poor planning can ruin your trip and cause stress or worse for your dog.

We have traveled with our dogs to many places over the years; from camping in the Cascades, staying in cabins by the wild Washington coast, Cross County drives to Glacier National Park and many visits with friends and family.

One camping trip was during the summer in northeast Washington and to ensure our dogs Herman and Zimbabwe stayed cool when we could not be with them we brought our horse trailer. This served as a great place to keep all of our stuff but it also provided a safe and cool place for the dogs when we parked and in camp. There was plenty of air and shade plus with fans the dogs stayed cool and safe even on the hottest days.

Being creative helps when caring for Fido.

At the ocean our favorite resort is Kalaloch; they allow and even cater to dogs. Like many hotels and resorts there is a pet fee each day so our daily expenses are higher but worth it to watch the Ridgebacks run and play on the beach.

The biggest factor that makes our trips positive is having enough time to expend the dogs' energy and knowing that the dogs are calm and well-mannered around other people and animals.

Does it Make Sense to Take Fido With You?

- Does Fido really want to go to Disneyland or visit your family?

- Will you have time for Fido?

- Will it stress out Fido more to go on the trip then staying at home or at a dog camp?

Is Fido Welcome?

- Confirm that Fido will be welcome before you travel.

- Where are you staying: hotels, motels, camping? Who are you traveling with: friends, family, business associates?

- Do they even allow for dogs where you are staying? Do they like dogs? Will your dog like them? Do they have pets? If so will they like your dog?

- Call ahead for any restrictions on animals before traveling. Do they accept dogs? Conduct an internet search on "pet friendly hotels". Things to consider are size and breed of dogs, time of year and ask for a room that is close to dog bathroom areas.

- Many camping parks will allow dogs in the camp ground but not on the beach, on the trails or other fun places where you will want to go. Make sure when you leave Fido at camp they are safe from heat, other campers and don't bark or annoy others.

Is Fido a Joy to be Around?

- Ensure that Fido is well trained and a joy for others to be around.

- Your welcome will be short lived if he is uncontrolled, aggressive, making messes or getting into things uninvited.

- Consider training well ahead of your trip and stay at family, friends or hotels near your home for practice weekends.

Flying With Fido

- Many small dogs travel on planes easily, bigger dogs must be in with the cargo.

- Small dogs that fit under the seat in pet bags or cases may do fine but they must be well behaved, potty trained and can handle the stress of flying and travel.

- When your dog flies cargo try to find an airline that specializes in dogs, get direct flights when possible and be sure that you are on the same planes as your dog.

- Pay attention to the time of year; if Fido must be in cargo, stay clear of really cold or hot weather periods.

- New pet only airlines are being started...so look into this as an option.

- If your dog must fly cargo, ask yourself if your trip is long enough for the risk and stress; otherwise find care for him at home, with a friend or with a professional.

- Veterinarian and health requirements are extensive for both the airline and possibly your destination. Check with your airline and do an online search for the current requirements for where you are flying to and from.

Remember you will need to get Fido back home after your trip so make sure you understand any requirements to get him back home. If you have any confusion or questions contact a professional animal transporter that has experience with regulations well before your trip.

Most dogs fly cargo, Wilhelm gets to fly in a Cessna

Car Travel With Fido

- Automobiles are the best way for traveling with Fido. Most dogs love to ride in the car, but some get motion sickness, so consider your individual dog.

- Some dogs do better sitting in a seat with a seat belt watching the sights; while others like being secure in their crate that is strapped tight.

- Make sure your dog likes longer car rides before heading out on long trips. If Fido has a hard time, start with shorter trips that always end up at a favorite location like the park, pet store or other fun place.

- If Fido must come on the trip and he has a tough time; ask your veterinarian about anti-anxiety medications or herbal supplements which may help him with travel.

- Stop every few hours at locations that are friendly for your dog. Not only for potty but also to run, stretch and drink water. Look for a fresh field and try not to use the rest stop dog areas where there is an overuse of traveling dogs. Look out for unleashed dogs in the area.

- What is the weather? Is it safe to leave your dog in the car when you eat or visit attractions? If this will be a concern consider leaving Fido at home or with professional care.

- Acquire a battery powered fan that can pull hot air out of the car and get a gage to know the temperature in your car while the engine is off. Park in parking garages that help keep the car cooler in the summer and warmer in the winter. Remember shade moves so don't trust parking in the shade for more than a few minutes.

Make Fido Welcome and Safe Once Settled

- Walk around the area when you get to your location. If possible walk for 45 - 60 minutes before settling into the new digs.

- Show Fido your accommodation and be clear what the rules are and where he can go and places that he is not allowed.

- Introduce Fido to friends, family, staff and other animals; have them give him a treat that you provide.

- Bring toys and bedding that has home and family smells.

- Provide special treats to reward good behavior.

- When possible use a crate or playpen for safety and security. This may be a larger crate than the one he traveled in, many fold up to a much smaller size for travel.

- If you need to do something where dogs are not allowed or it's not safe for Fido, what will you do with him? Will the hotel or friends let you keep him in your room? Are there local doggie day cares or overnight boarding facilities that you can use?

- Be prepared for emergencies; ask your veterinarian about having Benadryl for bee stings, spider bites or other allergies. Know where local veterinarians are and have their phone numbers handy. Know the sudden "signs of illness" and be prepared.

- Remember to clean up after Fido, keep baggies handy!

Hotel Travel

- More and more hotels and motels are pet friendly, but not all so make sure you know their rules before booking or bringing Fido.

- Some places charge a one-time extra cleaning fee and others charge per dog per day while the best may have a refundable damage deposit or no fee.

- Many will allow one or two small dogs, some total pounds of pup or pups and the best know that size and breed does not determine if they are good or bad guests.

- If Fido is any of the high profile breeds check to see if they have any breed restrictions.

- Some hotels are including pet perks like beds, treats and even special room service menus. Make sure you don't let Fido indulge in any new foods or you and him may be very unhappy.

- Desirable hotel traits; allowing dogs on beds and in the room while you are dining, rooms near pet walking areas and hotels near hiking trails and staff who knows how to approach dogs and provide local resources.

- If you do travel often with Fido and stay at hotels there are many books and web sites dedicated to this subject.

> **"More hotels are pet friendly, but not all...know their rules before bringing Fido."**

Safety First, Provide Extra Protection While Traveling

- Include many phone numbers on Fido's tag (Home, cell, friends, and family; anyone who will represent you if you are unavailable).

- Have two collars on Fido, one for tags and one to attach to your leash. This ensures your dog will still have ID if the collar somehow slips off your dog's neck while walking on lead. One idea is to use a bandanna and write your phone number in permanent ink.

- Martingales, gentle leaders, harnesses or prong collars provide extra safety while leash walking.

- Collars and tags are in addition to having a microchip on Fido: the tag allows people to find your number right away and does not require them to take your dog to the veterinarian or animal shelter to be scanned before they know your phone number.

- Some breeds like the Bullies are not always welcome in some towns; check local laws before visiting with your dog; even for a few hours.

- Keep Fido safe and secure while moving, either in a secured crate or with a seat belt.

- Don't allow Fido to have his head out the window, a small opening is enough for him to smell the world go by without having bugs or debris cause injury.

- Always keep Fido on a leash while traveling, even if he is good off leash, you and he do not know the area and the local hazards including other dogs.

- Take extra care for parasites and diseases such as heartworm, ticks, hookworms and fleas. Research the area you are visiting and determine if your dog needs additional protection, check with your vet if you are unsure. If the risk is too high for your dog's health, consider having him stay at home.

Health and Feeding

- Bring medications and supplements in original bottles in case of reactions or to get renewals; also have extra in case of travel delays.

- If Fido eats special food, either bring enough for entire trip or call stores ahead of time in the area to check to see if they have the same brand and version. If they don't have it, switch food weeks BEFORE to a brand that is available where you are traveling. Also bring a cutout of food ingredients in case you need to find a similar product.

- If feeding raw food, switching to dehydrated raw will make it easier for travel. You can always add fresh meat from the market to supplement.

- When driving, it helps to bring water from home to ensure Fido will drink and maintain a healthy tummy.

- Bring canned pumpkin and other tummy supplements to help with digestion issues.

- Bring medical, vaccination records and health certificates. Have extra copies in different suitcases.

When NOT to Bring Fido on Your Trip

🐾 If the car or airplane ride is too long for your dog.

🐾 If the weather is too hot or too cold and you cannot ensure their safety.

🐾 If Fido does not listen and needs training to make the trip successful.

🐾 If Fido won't get the attention that he deserves.

🐾 If Fido has health or emotional issues and traveling would be stressful.

🐾 If Fido is scared of new places or may be an escape risk, a boarding facility may be best for him.

🐾 If you are not certain that where you are staying will welcome him (don't assume your family or friends will want your dog in their home).

"Only bring Fido on your trip if you have time to make sure he is safe and well cared for."

Chapter 4
Dog Care Option #2

Leave Fido at Home, With a Friend or a Pet Sitter

There are many options for Fido if you decide to have him cared for at home or to take him to a friend's home.

The success of this route will depend on your dog's health, his activity level, his need to interact with other dogs, training, length of your trip and of course finding a caregiver that matches to your home and Fido.

I was fortunate as my Mom could help care for our dogs either at our home or at her home over the years. Having her stay at our ranch allowed her to care for the dogs, cats, horses and even weed the garden.

Once our dogs required special care, a professional was required to come to the ranch. This kept everyone at home until I decided that taking the dogs to a dog ranch was the best fit, now they get to be cared for with our other guests.

"One of our guests at the ranch, Buster, a happy easy going lab, is friends with Sam's retired neighbor Beth. As Beth already takes Buster out for an occasional walk and enjoys his company Buster stays with her when Sam travels. On the trips when she is busy, Buster comes to camp. Either way Sam knows that Buster is happy and enjoying himself when away from Dad."

Leave Fido at Home

- Many dogs will enjoy staying home in their own environment while others do better in an interactive dog facility.

- Will your caregiver be in the home all day and night, overnight or just for a few checks during the day?

- If you have more than one pet does everyone get along when you are not home?

- Double check your fencing and gates. Make sure your fence is tall enough and if you have invisible fences remember that they only keep your dog in but they do not keep others out.

- Think about your dog, what would he like best?

- Preparation generates a higher level of success.

- Caregivers can either be a professional pet sitter, a neighbor, family member or friend.

- Only have Fido stay home if you can ensure he gets enough care for his personal needs.

> "Many dogs will enjoy staying home in their own environment while others do better in an interactive dog facility."

Take Fido to a Friend's Home

- If you are thinking about leaving Fido at a friend's make sure your friend and their family like dogs and will have time to care for Fido.

  - Do they like dogs? I mean really like dogs? Does their spouse and kids like dogs?

  - Just because they like you does not mean they really like Fido.

- Are they dog savvy?

- Do they have children in the home?

- How long will the family be gone during the day?

- Do they have a busy social life?

- Where will your dog sleep?

- Where will your dog play, potty, go on walks? Is fencing secure?

- Does your friend have animals your dog will live with? Do they like or even know each other?

- Visit many times ahead of time so everyone knows each other in this setting; consider an overnight to see how things go.

Ensure Fido Likes The Caregivers

- Does your dog know and like the caregivers and any family members they will come in contact with?

- Is your dog confident enough to come to your caregiver?

- If Fido gets scared or is dominating with others, confirm that your caregiver knows how to approach him without triggering aggression or fear.

- Has Fido ever bitten or nipped anyone? Has he ever come close to biting anyone? Provide all caregivers his history and if biting or nipping was based on fear or dominance and what may trigger it in the future...if there is concern then ensure only professionals care for Fido, safety first!

Plan For Emergencies

- Have an emergency plan for weather or other emergencies.

- What happens if there is snow, heat wave, power outage, freeze, illness, emergency or a natural disaster...can your caregiver get to your dog and ensure all is well?

- Enlist a "kind" neighbor who knows that Fido is staying inside a house if events will cause your caregiver to be delayed.

- Provide a backup caregiver. If something does happen to your caregiver for whatever reason have an emergency contact or other pet care choice as a backup; provide their contact information to the "kind" neighbor so they can be reached.

Will Caregivers Have Time For Fido?

- Ask what the schedule will be like, will Fido be a burden or will they have time for all your dog's needs?

- If Fido is left inside, will they have access to a potty area or will the caregivers come early enough and then late enough for the final potty break?

- Will there be time for walks away from eating? For some large, energetic or barrel chested breeds ensure all active walks are 30 – 60 minutes before and after eating. This will reduce bloating and other internal issues. Remember the saying, "no swimming 30 minutes before or after eating"; the same rule should be applied for dogs.

- If Fido is at a friend's home, will children be coming home before the adults? If so ensure your dog knows the kids well, that the kids have strict rules for interaction with Fido and all will be safe.

Yard Safety

- Check all play area fences and gates; even at your own home Fido may try to explore when you are away.

- Some dogs have the ability to climb up fence wire like a ladder so know your dog's skills.

- Limit the amount of time Fido is outside to keep him from getting into trouble.

- Confirm or add security locks/latches to all gates and when possible have a double gate system.

- Know when utility people are checking gages or if you have any yard services ensure they are not opening gates when Fido is alone in the yard.

- Add signs that you have a dog in the yard to the gate latches for extra safety. People may not read signs on a gate but they will if the sign is attached to the lock or latch. If people use multi languages in your area include them in your sign.

- Remember that just because Fido does not jump a 4 foot fence at home does not mean he won't in a new place or if you are gone for long periods.

"Sammy a shy scared smaller lab mix has a 3 foot fence at home, when his mom had him stay at a friends she thought their 4 foot fence was secure enough for him. After a few days being cared for by the friend a thunder storm developed and when backs were turned Sammy leaped right over the fence, after a few hours searching he was found safe and sound. Now Sammy's mom knows that he only stays in his fence because he wants to, not because it's secure. Consider your dog's ability for future escapes and not that he has not gotten out in the past."

Health and Feeding

- Does Fido require any medication, shots, supplements or other special needs? Confirm caregivers are able to support any special requirements.

- Keep medication/supplements in original bottles in case of reactions or renewals; have extra in case of travel restrictions or emergencies.

- Provide enough of Fido's current food for the entire trip, bring a cutout of food ingredients in case a similar product is needed for any reason.

- Provide tummy aids to help with digestion: pumpkin, yogurt, probiotics, and over the counter supplements.

- Ask your veterinarian about what first aid ideas to have on hand like Benadryl in case of allergies, bee stings or spider bites.

- Confirm your caregiver can administer special foods, supplements and medications if needed.

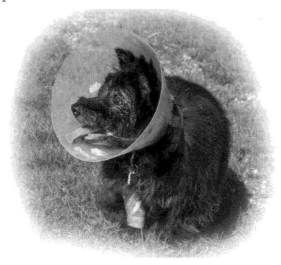

Illness or Injury

- Have a plan if the worst happens; Fido gets sick or is hurt.

- Provide all veterinarian information, Fido's history; your contact information and friends or family living nearby to help with any decisions if you are unavailable.

- Talk with caregivers on how much you are able to spend on any emergencies; it's a hard discussion but a needed one. Don't place the burden of making a tough decision on their shoulders.

- Provide a credit card or give one to another friend who the caregiver can contact.

- Confirm the caregiver knows what veterinarian to contact if they need to, both during regular hours and during evenings, nights or weekends.

- If possible use your regular veterinarian, but if distance is an issue pick another close to the caregiver before your trip. Provide your credit card information to the veterinarian.

- Have a check list for the caregiver with all veterinarians, friends, your contacts and full instructions to ensure they know what to do in an emergency; your backup caregivers and your neighbors should have the same list.

> **"Have a plan if the worst happens; Fido gets sick or is hurt."**

At Home Or With Friend, Caregivers To Consider

Family Or Friends

🐾 Good choice if they have time and know your dog well.

🐾 It is better if they are retired but don't overlook your working friends.

🐾 Many older people love having a dog around without the long term responsibility, however consider physical limitations with a big dog who may pull.

🐾 May not work well if Fido has special needs or if other pets are in the home.

🐾 Does your dog respect your friend and does your friend know how to respect and care for Fido?

Adult or Teenager Neighbor

🐾 May already know your dog well.

🐾 If a teen, have the parents know the plan, process and monitor.

🐾 Can be a good choice if your dog is healthy and easy to care for.

🐾 Elderly dog loving neighbors would be a great choice if they can handle your dog's physical needs.

At Home Or With Friend, Caregivers To Consider

Young Adult

- Family, friends or neighbors.
- Many older teens or early 20's are available between school terms if in collage.
- Good choice for in-home overnight care.
- Have another adult check to make sure all is well.
- Vet tech or other animal care worker.
- Check their background and get referrals.

Professional Pet Sitter or Dog Walker

- Professional pet care providers know how to care for many different animals, personalities and health issues; this is their love and joy.
- Many pet professionals visit for limited time periods. Remember they are traveling around caring for many animals.
- Some stay overnight, many do not as they have their own home and animals to care for.
- Some pet sitters have a staff of pet caregivers while others are independent and do the animal care themselves. When scheduling ask who will be the individual coming to the home and caring for your dog. Know you may not get to choose who is caring for your dog.

- Professionals normally have liability insurance while friends and neighbors do not, this will help with any problems that could arise.

- If your pet professional has a logo on their vehicle neighbors may know you are out of town.

- Finding a pet sitter – same as finding other professional animal care; ask your local pet store, veterinarians, groomers, dog trainer, friends and co-workers. You can also search online through the "National Association of Professional Pet Sitters" or "Pet Sitters International".

- Check references of all caregivers.

- Many pet sitters offer walks, hikes, trips to the veterinarian, dog park visits. These outings are important for an active dog and when you are gone longer than a few days.

- Cost of pet sitters: after finding a pet sitter that you are interested in, make sure to discuss fees and policies.

- Confirm that you are both in agreement of your expectations and what they can provide including amount of time spent at your home and with Fido each visit.

- Go over all services you are thinking about and get an estimate. Most pet sitters have a base fee for each trip to the house then additional fees for each extra service like watering plants, getting mail and caring for multiple animals.

Professional Pet Sitter or Dog Walker (continued)

- 🐾 Some pet sitters require 2 or 3 visits a day for dog care while cat care just once a day.

- 🐾 Tipping is always nice, especially if the pet sitter is not the owner.

- 🐾 All pet sitters should have you fill out contact information, history forms and sign a contract. Similar to what you would sign for a boarding facility.

- 🐾 Have the pet sitter come to the home ahead of the trip so you can review the home, meet Fido and go over all tasks. Keep all emergency and contact phone numbers out where it's easy to see.

> **"Professional Pet Sitters or Dog Walkers know how to care for many types of animals, personalities and health issues; this is their love and joy"**

When NOT To Use Friends Or Family; Consider a Professional Dog Care Giver

🐾 If your dog needs extra care for many reasons your friends may not have "dog" experience to care for them properly.

🐾 When asking friends to care for your dog may be too much for the "friendship" or for your pup.

🐾 If your dog would worry being left at home without his family being home.

🐾 If your dog would be better off with one of the choices listed in the following chapters.

🐾 If you want your dog to have training, new experiences or have his own vacation while you are on your trip.

🐾 If the trip is long and Fido would enjoy an interactive dog camp or pet hotel.

Chapter 5
Dog Care Option #3

Take Fido To a Professional Pet Hotel, Dog Ranch, Dog Boarding Kennel or Pet Care Center

There are many types of professional boarding facilities with many different services and descriptions.

From custom dog ranches, upscale pet hotels, doggie resorts or pet care centers where Fido gets pampered for his every whim, to the commercial traditional dog kennel where the dogs are kept in individual kennels most or all of the day and night. Sizes range from over 500+ animals to under 10 for smaller home style places with many care centers in the middle.

No matter the name or marketing you need to review each facility and make sure they match to your dog's individual needs and your family's wishes.

Why You Should Consider Taking Your Dog To Professional Dog Care Facilities

Boarding professionals design and operate their various Pet Care Centers to specifically care for your animal while you travel or for other times when Fido needs a home away from home. Their goal is to provide Fido with excellent pet care and peace of mind for you.

While taking your dog to a facility may be stressful the first time, many people find they enjoy seeing how much fun their dog has at camp when the type of environment matches Fido's personality.

Extra Services May Help Fido Have Fun or Provide Further Learning

Many dog boarding places provide a variety of pet services such as overnight boarding, doggie-daycare, grooming, training, holistic healing, spa services and some even provide pet supplies.

Thinking dogs such as Border Collies like to use their brains, hunting dogs need that extra time for searching or playing ball and most dogs could use some extra training. If your dog is older or has health issues a massage could help with the additional stress of being away from family.

Some services to ask about are:

- Community play with other dogs.

- Additional personalized play and walks.

- Training for obedience, calmness, being around other dogs or agility, full board and train.

- New experiences around horses, sheep, chickens.

- Therapy for body, mind or spirit with massages, rieki, water therapy.

- Extra grooming, nail trims or bathing.

- Help with shipping if you are moving.

Type of People Who Run or Work at or Own a Professional Dog Care Facility

People who work in the dog fields normally have a deep respect and love for animals and their main motivation is ensuring the health and happiness of your dog.

Most have an understanding of dog behavior and have a natural ability which is important for places where dogs play with other guests. Skills include interpreting dog body language and how to prevent and break up disputes or fights.

Professional animal caregivers are trained to recognize distress and illness that family or friends may mistake as laziness or depression.

Dogs may have tummy or intestinal conditions, loss of appetite or other illness that a qualified caretaker recognizes and know to seek veterinary assistance as needed. Most professional pet care givers are around the animals for most if not all of the day and can see slight changes in the dogs to determine if there are any signs of illness.

While many animal care givers know dogs, as in every field; there may be people who are not well suited for the task. So don't assume every professional is a good fit, so ask questions and go with your gut feeling.

Cost of Professional Dog Boarding Facilities

The cost to care for one dog ranges anywhere from $15 a day for a traditional or commercial kennel in rural areas up to $80 a day or more for some pet resorts.

An average is in the range of $30 - $60 a day for one dog and many provide discounts for multiple dogs and caring for other animals.

If money is tight look at the options in chapter 2 and you can always ask about discounts or special rates for health reasons or the elderly.

Some facilities will have a lower daily rate and charge for each activity like group play, walks or treat time; other places have a flat rate and only charge extra for training, therapy or special excursions. Price will also depend on your location within the country.

> "Don't assume every professional pet care giver is a good fit, ask your questions and go with your gut feeling."

Planning Your Trip

- Conduct your research and make a list of candidate facilities months ahead if possible.

    - Make a list of your priorities from must haves to nice features.

    - Are you looking for a "home away from home" for all future trips, or for this one trip?

- Contact the facilities you are interested in and see if they have availably and to schedule tours.

    - Discuss your dog's individual needs. Can they provide the care you desire? Ask some basic questions to see if a visit is worth your time.

- Visit and see how the dogs are cared for before you schedule or confirm your reservation. You may want to schedule with the understanding that it is dependent upon the tour.

- If you don't have time for a tour make sure you have references from those you trust.

- Know that certain times of the year are busy and you will need to schedule ahead of time, sometimes months ahead. These include all holidays but also any weeks where your local schools are on vacation.

- One thing even childless folks should consider is school vacation schedules. Not only for dog care, but also for hotels and crowds. Keep in mind schedules vary in different parts of the country and around the world. Contact your hotel for specific information if you want to schedule away from kids vacations.

How to Find The Perfect Facility

- Know your commute range. Consider driving 30 – 90 minutes to increase your choices or if you want a country setting and you live in the city.

- Ask for recommendations by your veterinarian, pet store, rescue group, animal shelter, dog trainer, dog walker, doggie daycare, dog groups, dog play areas, and of course friends, family and coworkers.

  - Local small pet stores and veterinarians hear about the best care in the area and they often have a section or a book that includes cards and brochures for many pet services. Also check out their web page for referral businesses.

  - Co-workers and internal corporate pet clubs may have a great referral system.

  - Check with your local Chamber of Commerce.

  - On-line pet clubs and Facebook and other social media are a good start if you have enough members or friends in your local area.

- Have an idea of the type of pet care center you are interested in. Review the following pages and determine if you would like a dog ranch or resort, a large commercial dog kennel, a small family home or many of the other type of facilities.

- Also can your dog be mixed with other guests or will they need to have private space or a combination of the two?

- Conduct internet searches with Bing, Google, Yahoo and other search sites:

  - Suggested search words include your local area/city/town plus the various dog care synonyms. Examples include "dog boarding Seattle"; "dog care Redmond Washington"; "Everett dog hotel"; "best pet care in Tacoma". Expand your search by putting in towns near your area.

  - Local business map sites like Google Places are good but they may not highlight connecting towns and areas that could be better choices and are still in your driving range; just scroll over or use neighboring towns in your search words.

  - Best to first check the organic listings in your search results, the results on the right and top shaded areas are paid ads.

  - You-Tube has many businesses that show mini videos highlighting their facilities and knowledge. You-Tube also has an excellent search tool to help you find great care.

  - Review internet sites like: Yelp, findpetcare.com, dogboarding.com, insiderpages.com, angieslist.com, citysearch.com, merchantcircle.com, plus many other great pet and business sites.

  - A business may or may not have membership in the Better Business Bureau as they require a monthly fee and a business may choose not to join for many reasons.

- Search in Facebook for local business fan pages, again use search words like "Seattle Dog Care" or "Dog Boarding" in the search field.

- Check out your other favorite dog care business web sites and see if they have a referral page (vets, groomers, pet stores, pet sitters, dog daycare, and even some boarding businesses refer each other).

Go Beyond The Marketing

Marketing does not always provide the reality of the facility, it's easy to put up a nice web site or print great brochures. Marketing should include photos or videos of the pet care center and not just pictures of dogs playing. You want to see the play area and sleeping areas where Fido will be staying.

Look for reviews and testimonials on their web site and on local search review sites. Keep in mind that most people who write reviews are either really happy, very unhappy, a friend or even the competition; so use them as just one reference point.

Sometimes just talking to the potential caregivers gives you a good sense of whether or not you would want to consider having Fido stay with them. The next step is a live visit.

Tour Possible Pet Care Centers Before You Make Your Final Decision

Scheduling Your Visit

- Call ahead, discuss your dog's individual needs, can they provide the care you desire? Ask some basic questions to see if a trip is even worth your time.

- Bring Fido if possible; it helps them to come, sniff and then go home.

- Most of the smaller places require you make an appointment so they will have time; larger facilities may be able to accommodate drop-ins. If you come unannounced you may need to wait for the staff to have time for a tour as they are busy caring for the guest dogs or helping other clients.

- Some of the free-range/cage-free places require a pre-visit to make sure your dog matches to their other guests while other facilities will work with each dog's individual needs and may not require a pre-visit.

Are You Welcome?

- Large facilities may have a check-in desk while smaller places may not.

- Smaller places usually have less staff available. If they are busy you may need to wait for incoming or outgoing dogs before they will have time for your visit.

- How is your dog greeted? Does he feel welcome?

Dogs Health and Happiness

- Do the dog guests seem happy and well cared for?
- How often are the dogs checked, played with or walked?
- What is the process if your dog refuses to eat?
- What is the process if your dog gets diarrhea or is vomiting?
- Will they feed food provided by you or do they feed their own brand?
- If you feed homemade, raw or special diets can they support your request?
- What is the process to ensure dogs with food allergies are not given inappropriate food?
- What steps are taken when a dog is aggressive towards other dogs/people or if they are afraid to be left alone?
- Ask the number of dogs per caregiver, this will be dependent upon type of facility and type of dogs. A rule of thumb is about 1 person for every 10 – 15 dogs for every eight hour shift, more staff if the dogs are special needs or they handle many different types of dogs.
- Do the animal care takers know to look for signs of distress or illness?
- What happens when a dog gets sick, what veterinarians are available, where will they take your dog if they are ill or for emergencies? Will they contact you if there is an emergency or any concern?
- Can the care center support special needs for your dog?

Review Where Fido Will sleep and Rest

- Pet care centers have many different layouts for housing dogs; some provide indoor rooms or crates and use outside play exercise areas; other kennels are indoor/outdoor traditional runs and there are even some that provide group sleep areas.

- Make sure you know the advantages of the system and confirm it supports your dog's needs.

- Check that the rooms are large enough for the type and health of your dog. Active dogs need space to play and older pups need enough to spread out and to move around to keep their joints flexible.

- If dogs are sleeping with other guest dogs ask how they ensure the safety of the dogs.

- If you have more than one dog can they share a room, do they have limits on the number of dogs from the same family? Do they limit mixing your dogs if they are different sizes?

- Check the room design, many rooms will have solid walls for privacy while others are more of the traditional wire kennels; is there some type of divider and a private place for your dog to sleep and feel secure from other guest dogs?

- If your dog is a climber or jumper make sure rooms and runs are secure with tops or are inside. Consider a crate if your dog is a security risk.

- Does the facility provide bedding? Can you bring your own? Make sure Fido will not be sleeping on hard surfaces and that all bedding is clean and comfortable.

- If dogs are kept in crates make sure your dog is crate trained before your trip and the dogs are out most of the day; if your dog does not like crates find another facility.

- Ask where the dogs are expected to use the bathroom. Outside, in their room/run or other indoor area.

- Do they have music, radio or TV to help the dogs?

Daily Schedule

- Ask how often and how long the dogs get exercise, play and potty breaks. What is the daily schedule your dog can expect? Make sure they are walked and played with for their age and type.

  Typical Mystic Mountain Pet Retreat Schedule:
  - AM potty break & breakfast about 7:30–9:00am
  - Rest 9:00 – 10:00 am
  - Play/walks between 10:00 – 5:00
  - Dinner between 5:00 – 6:00pm
  - Evening potty and treat break about 9:30 pm
  - Always a rest right after eating to digest food and before for barrel chested dogs.
  - Minimum of 5 outings per day, usually about 7
  - Play periods average about 30 - 45 minutes each, with at least 4 hours outside on nice days... most dogs will be out much longer unless older or special needs.

  - Each pet care center's schedule will vary; the above is just one example.

- Ask when the last and first potty break is for your dog, do they have to wait more than 10 hours overnight?

- Ensure your dog will get out at least 3 times each day; the optimum time is more like 5-7 times during the day or all day play (with some rest periods).

Community Play, Exercise and Supervision

- All dogs should get some type of exercise to support their size, breed, activity level, age, health and mind. Ask what activities are available for Fido. If the dog care center does not provide enough walks, play or other activities only consider the facility if your stay is for a night or two and if you can't find another care option.

- For older, special needs or even high energy dogs make sure the activity level is monitored to ensure Fido does not get over exercised, stressed, cause undo weight loss or becomes injured.

- Will Fido get to play with other dogs? Are they used to playing with strange dogs? Most dogs enjoy play and being social, confirm the attendants know how to monitor for individual needs and stress level in a community play scenario. If you don't want your dog to play with others make sure they are not mixed and that they are walked or played with independently.

- Community play or recreational play groups should be grouped by size, age, energy and the individual personality; be wary of places that group ALL guest dogs together unless they are prescreened or they know them well. Ask how the dogs are grouped and how many dogs per group per dog care attendant.

- Dogs will change over time, just because they do well in an all free range environment does not mean they will always enjoy it. Ask what happens if a dog is having a bad day or does not like a specific guest? Confirm that the facility can separate the dogs when needed. Will they call you if there are any issues?

- Ask how the caregivers deal with dog disagreements or fights and what the protocol is when an injury occurs.

- If the facility has all day play ask what they do to keep the dogs from getting cranky or stressed by the other dogs, do the dogs have rest periods? What happens if it's raining, snowing, cold or hot? Nap times should be part of the daily schedule, this is important not only for older dogs but also for the high energy dog who do not know how to stop playing.

- Ask where and how often the dogs potty; If they are required to go in their kennel or other inside area consider finding another facility. What is their process for when the dogs are constipated or have diarrhea.

- Some places will have internet cameras so you can see Fido while you travel; if the place is smaller or at a private home they may not want to have the world view their place for personal or for security reasons. Remember if you can see your dog at the ranch then so can anyone checking to see if you are on vacation.

- Community play all day with group sleeping may be called "Cage Free" or "Free Range" boarding. While this setup works for some dogs not all enjoy being with other dogs they don't know well 24/7. Also constant interaction may be stressful and can keep dogs in an aroused energy which may cause for disagreements and overall physical distress. Ask if the dogs have nap-time, are able to be separated out if needed, the feeding setup and if there is supervision while dogs are mixed even at night.

Pet Care Givers

- Do the caregivers seem knowledgeable and caring? Are they friendly and calm around the dogs? Do they take the time to answer your questions? Do they seem to know how to care for the dogs?

- Ask how many hours the caregivers are with the dogs each day. Ask how many dogs per caregivers each day.

- Is there someone on the property outside of the normal care hours? It's best to have someone living or staying overnight, just know that if you choose a smaller facility the caretakers may leave for a few hours to run errands, take dogs out on hikes, go to the vet or just out to dinner.

- Many larger facilities or vets may not have anyone on the property overnight; if this is the case ask about fire detection, sprinkler systems and emergency plans.

Cleaning and Building Health

- Does the facility look and smell clean?

- What cleaning solutions do they use and how often...not only rooms/kennels but how is the play field cleaned? (Natural products for normal cleaning work well and for full cleaning either Bleach, WASHIEZ or another heavy cleaner is needed for complete sterilization)

- Check that the facility has appropriate temperatures. Are they heated or require air conditioning? If not, ask how cold or hot it gets during extreme weather and how they ensure the safety, comfort and happiness of the dogs.

- Is the building properly ventilated, free of offensive odors with good air circulation?

- How secure is the facility? Confirm the fencing supports your dog's needs.

- Check that all dogs have clean water bowls and ask how often the bowls are washed and refreshed.

- Is the area and rooms free of sharp edges and harmful chemicals?

- Ask about their fire and smoke detection, equipment and prevention.

- The area should be clean and no accumulation of fecal matter.

Emergencies

- Do they have backup generators during power failures? If not, what is their plan?

- Are there caregivers nearby during the night? If not, what fire detection, sprinkler systems and emergency service is provided?

- What is the facility's emergency and evacuation plan for fires, flooding, power outages, snow, heat wave...

- If there is snow or other storms, do they have enough staff to care for the animals?

- If the roads are hard to access, do they have backup plans to get and return Fido if you can't access their location?

Requirements and Policies

- Ask what types of vet records, forms and history are required.

- Ask the facilities what their requirements are for vaccinations and worming control. Requirements will vary depending on your location in the country, your vets recommendations, your own vaccination beliefs, the size of the facility and the individual kennels rules.

- What are the policies for flea and tick prevention? If the facility automatically gives all pets entering or leaving a flea bath or treatment, ensure they don't use any products your dog may have a reaction to, this is very important for older, sick or special needs dogs.

- Do they have the required business and kennel licenses for your area?

- What type of training do the caregivers have? First aid? Dog behavior skilled in dog body language?

Facilities & Pet Care Centers to Walk Away From

- If you would not want to stay there then don't leave Fido.

- All the workers are teenagers, it is ok for some but there should be caregivers with experience and maturity.

- The dogs are going crazy and the place does not seem to be organized.

- Does not have someone on the property overnight without security and safety systems.

  - It may be a surprise to know that some boarding places, including vets are not staffed 24/7.

  - Large facilities should have 24/7 care. Smaller dog ranches or home care should have people on the property most of the time; with breaks for hikes, errands or going out for dinner.

- Does not ask about your dog's medical, vaccination or parasite history.

- Does not ask about your dog's emotional and social history.

- Does not ask for your dog's veterinarian name and contact information.

- Does not support your dog's specific diet or other special needs.

- Does not provide daily exercise and potty breaks away from their sleeping area.

- Is unclean, has dirty water or smells without a reason.

- Does not allow you to see all areas of the facility (at least a quick look from the door, health and safety may require some areas to be restricted).

- Does not show you proper licenses for your area.

- Does not provide a safe and comfortable climate controlled environment.

- Does not handle the dogs with care and love.

Considerations

For new places have Fido stay overnight or visit about 2 – 4 weeks before your trip.

- Important for rescue dogs.

- Important for long trips.

- Fido will know he is going home after visiting the place.

- Helps Fido to overcome separation anxiety and enjoy their vacation.

- May not be needed if Fido is confident and used to visiting different places.

Bring Fido's blankets and toys to connect him to you and home.

- Make sure to bring items that you don't mind getting lost, dirty or destroyed.

- Don't wash the blankets just before the trip to keep the home smells embedded. Make sure they have no fleas.

- If Fido doesn't have a blanket or bed, you can always put an old towel in your bed for a night.

- If you are going for a long trip, put towels with your scent sealed in bags that can be brought out every week or so.

- Label your items when possible and provide a list of your items.

- Some places won't allow for personal items. This may be due to either being a large facility or because the dogs are free-range and could cause them to be possessive or get into disputes with other dogs.

Have Fido wear a flat collar with tags or phone numbers including friends or family written on the collar. Provide chip info in case of escape.

Keep Fido on his own diet and don't indulge in new treats the week before and after you travel.

- Stay away from places that want to feed your dog the facilities food, this is only easier for the staff and may be stressful for your dog's digestion causing diarrhea or vomiting.

- Again NO feeding of foods that your dog is not used to just before and after your trip.

- Provide something healthy to enhance your dog's food in case they are not eating well.

- For overall healthy digestion think about rotating Fido's diet with different meat and grain type dog foods months ahead of any trips; and even add healthy homemade foods to their daily feeding.

When possible provide all medical treatments weeks BEFORE or AFTER your trip as they cause some stress to the body and soul.

- Vaccinations require more than a few days to mount an adequate antibody response against the disease... also any reactions may take a few days and you want Fido to be home where you can see any changes in their behavior.

- Coordinate with your veterinarian and let them know when you are planning a trip so that treatments can be scheduled away from the trip time if at all possible.

Mark all medications and supplements with Fido's name and full instructions.

- If Fido is taking medication, supplements or has a special diet ask if they can support your needs. Many facilities will not accept excessive care, specific time of administration or types of medication. Ask if there are any additional fees for the extra care.

- Bring Fido's medicine bottles in case they need to be refilled or reviewed with a vet or if you are delayed.

- Setting up daily pill boxes helps the caregiver confirm that all pills are administered.

- For items requiring cooling or freezing, confirm the facility has a fridge and freezer.

- If your dog requires injections, confirm the facility can support this extra procedure; if they say it's no problem, make sure they know how to administer the injection, the amount given, if the medicine needs to be kept cold or other special requirements. Be certain the specific staff members that will be working with your pup on the days and times injections are needed are also trained to provide injections.

- If the medicine should be administered every 12 hours ask if the facility can support the timing. Breakfast and dinner may be spaced closer to 8 -10 hours...if this is the case, can someone give your dog's medications close to the 12 hours separation?

- If the medicine/supplement needs to be administered away from food; make sure they are able to support this requirement.

Bring extra supplies in case of delays coming home.

- You never know when there are natural disasters, snow storms or airline strikes.

- At least provide enough medications and special food for a few days and into the mid-week to enable caregivers to purchase extra supplies or contact veterinarians.

- Never have your medications or special food run out on a weekend even if you are planning to be home.

Review your flea and tick protection plan

- If using chemicals use name-brand products like "Advantage" and "Frontline"; apply at least days or one week ahead. Consider only using if its flea season.

- Natural flea control includes: healthy immune system with diet, yeast and garlic; removing fleas with combs and natural soaps; home prevention with beneficial nematodes outside and diatomaceous earth inside.

- Some places require chemical protection while others allow holistic prevention, know the requirements and make sure it works with your dog's health.

- Know that it's tough to be 100% flea free 100% of the time where many dogs live so be prepared to protect your dog and if the facility is natural don't get upset if they pick up a flea or two; check at pickup and give a bath if needed.

- Older dogs and those with health issues may be a target for fleas and should be closely checked.

Business Details

- All responsible professionals will have you fill out a history form that includes owner information, veterinarian information, health, diet, emotional and behavior backgrounds for Fido. Once you have stayed at a facility, you should be filling out an Every Trip form that includes updates and specific trip information.

- A Boarding Agreement or Contract that outlines your rights and responsibilities and the kennels responsibilities and legal limitations is important.

- Make sure you are clear about the rates and fees for your dog. Many places charge an extra night or add a day fee if you checkout after a specific time. Some places charge by the day and others charge by the night. Know if your dog will be receiving any additional services that will be charged.

- Know the payment process: prepayment at drop-off, or at pickup or a deposit with the remainder due at pickup. What type of payment is accepted? Many small places do not take credit cards while other places may not take checks; most accept cash.

- If the worst happens, do they require a credit card for veterinarian emergencies, confirm they have clear instructions on what procedures you want or don't want your dog to have and of how much you can spend.

- Make sure you or your emergency contacts are communicated with for any issues, health or vet care.

- Some health care will need to be addressed right away by a vet and if you are unavailable the facility may need to make decisions on your behalf, for other health issues waiting for your input may be advisable.

- If your dog is older, you may not want complicated procedures. Don't feel bad about having a limit on the cost of veterinarian care. The minimum care that should be provided for all dogs in distress is fluids, exam and pain management.

- The hours of operation for pickups and drop-offs are different for each facility. Know their hours and if they can be flexible outside of the regular hours if needed, never show up outside of open hours without prior arrangements.

- Shuttle or taxi service may be offered by the facility or by a partnering service to help when you have a busy schedule.

  - If this is your first time using the facility, you may want to drop-off and pick up your pup to help with the experience.

  - When you personally pick up Fido you will see firsthand how your dog is doing and his energy level. (Example, if your dog comes home stressed from a taxi you won't know if it's the taxi or the kennel)

- Each state and county has different requirements for licensing and certification and even if a facility meets the current codes; that does not mean that the kennel is a place where you want to leave your dog.

  - Kennel licensing is a baseline of care and you will need to do your own visit and inspection.

- There are many kennel, pet care or pet sitting memberships and certifications. Some only require a membership fee while others require the facility or person to meet specific requirements before earning a seal or certification. Ask the facility detailed questions and again use your eyes, ears and nose and do your own review or rely on trusted referrals from veterinarians, pet stores, and friends.

- When you are traveling far away or with no access to phones or email it's extra important to have friends or family represent you in case of your dog's illness or injury. Confirm they know what measures to take if needed and how much you are able to spend for veterinarian care.

- If you don't have someone you trust, be sure you, the facility and your veterinarian have this worked out. This is even more important if your dog is older or has special needs.

Types of Professional Pet Care Center Options

Dog Ranch or Camp - Boarding at a dog ranch, pet hotel, luxury pet resort, spa and retreat whose primary function is to provide overnight care for animals by the night, weeks or months with custom care.

Considerations:

- 🐾 Many have outdoor environment with fresh air and grass.

- 🐾 May require a longer drive for those living near the cities or suburbs.

- 🐾 Many different sleeping setups; some have separate indoor rooms, outside kennels, open group sleeping or utilize crates. Ask for the details.

- 🐾 Ask if the play is all day free range/group play or do they provide separate smaller community play with rest in-between. Can they support caring for your dog if your dog does not like some of the other guests or if another dog does not like them?

- 🐾 Additional services may include personalized play and walks, training, new experiences, massages or more.

- 🐾 Many support special needs or other individual requirements.

Types of Professional Pet Care Center Options

Day Care - Boarding at a doggie day care facility whose primary function is to offer "dog daycare" with limited overnight care.

Considerations:

- 🐾 Each facility has different overnight sleeping setups; some use crates, some suites, some kennels while others may have group sleeping.

- 🐾 Lots of dogs during the day which may be of benefit or stressful depending on your own dog and if they like large groups.

- 🐾 Some daycares are in large indoor warehouse facilities.

- 🐾 Good choice if this is your dog's day care for shorter trips. For longer trips consider a dog ranch or resort.

Professional Home - Boarding in a private professional home with a limited number of dogs.

Considerations:

- 🐾 Normally a small amount of dogs with a family lifestyle.

- 🐾 Normally requires your dog to do well in a group setting.

- 🐾 Ask what happens when the family or person is busy/sick/family emergency; do they bring in extra help?

- 🐾 Is the house and yard secure for your dog?

- 🐾 If your dog has special needs are there stairs, steps or slick floors?

- 🐾 If Fido does not do well with the family or other guests do they have a safe and comfortable place for him?

Types of Professional Pet Care Center Options

Veterinarian - Boarding at the veterinarian whose primary function is to care for sick animals.

Considerations:

- 🐾 Not all vets offer this service.

- 🐾 Convenient for many people.

- 🐾 Great if Fido needs medical care or monitoring.

- 🐾 Many veterinarians use cages or small kennels.

- 🐾 Fido could be around sick animals or personnel who also care for sick animals.

- 🐾 The potty area may also be used by sick animals or they must go in kennels, ask their policy.

- 🐾 Possibly a good choice for a night or two but consider an interactive place for longer stays.

Kennel –Boarding at a large traditional commercial kennel.

Considerations:

- 🐾 Typically less expensive than custom care facilities.
- 🐾 Many are closer to the city and have longer service hours.
- 🐾 Perhaps a good choice for aggressive/dominate dogs or for dogs who can't or don't want to mix with other dogs.
- 🐾 Many provide grooming, baths other services.
- 🐾 Most charge extra for treats, walks, play sessions, love, medications, or special foods.
- 🐾 Some places require dogs to potty inside the kennel, inside area or limited outside time.
- 🐾 Normally high level of barking which can be scary for some dogs.
- 🐾 Higher vaccination requirements due to the large number of dogs in their care.
- 🐾 May not allow for home bedding, toys or your dog's food.
- 🐾 Possibly a good choice for short stays but consider an interactive place for longer trips.

When NOT To Use a Professional Pet Care Center Boarding Facility

- 🐾 If Fido totally freaks out if left away from home and you don't have time to train him for a new place; a professional pet sitter in your home may be the best choice.

- 🐾 If Fido is aggressive to the handlers unless they are trained and have proper processes and facilities to ensure the safety of all; you may not be able to leave home if this is your dog.

- 🐾 If Fido gets so car sick that he cannot handle the drive to a facility.

- 🐾 If you can't find a good facility or person who can provide for your dog's specific needs, including health, emotional or behavior issues.

"If Fido totally freaks out, is aggressive or gets car sick a professional pet sitter in your home may be the best choice unless you can find a facility that specializes with your dog's needs."

Chapter 6

Getting Ready For Your Trip, Dropping Off and Picking Up Fido

Now that you have determined the best type of care for Fido you want to assure that he has a successful experience away from home. It's up to you to help him feel confident and secure getting ready, on the drive and when you pick him up from a Pet Care Center or Dog Care Provider.

Once you find a favorite pet care provider make reservations early, even before booking your flight or finalizing your plans. Having Fido stay at a familiar place will make the trip easier for you and him.

Early Training

- Provide Fido with new experiences during his life; expose him to as many different environments as possible like hardware stores, pet stores, busy streets, dog parks, trails, people, kids and other dogs. (Remember safety first!)

- Provide basic obedience training as a trained and well-mannered dog will have more options for overnight care; from traveling with you or more willing friends and even happier professional pet care givers.

- Have Fido used to playing with other dogs; either at the dog park, with friends, neighbors' pups or at doggie daycare.

- Get Fido used to being away from home at an early age. Start by taking him places when you travel, have friends care for him overnight and include a couple of overnight trips at a dog boarding facility. Life and emergencies may cause you to need Fido to stay away from home with little notice so having a place picked out and tested will help you and Fido.

Weeks Before The Trip

- If this is Fido's first time boarding or even if it's the first time at a new facility then have him visit or stay a few nights before the trip. This is more to help him get ready or for you to have time to work out any problems before the trip then to see if the facility is a perfect match. Some dogs need a few times seeing and smelling the place then going home so they know it's just a vacation and not being abandoned.

- If possible take Fido to many different places like the park, hardware stores, pet stores with different smells, people and other dogs. Consider enrolling in a day care to help with socialization. This will give him confidence when staying in a new environment.

- Brushing up on basic commands and social skills will help your dog be mixed with other dogs and not left alone.

- Visit your veterinarian for a health check and nail trimming. If any procedures are required it is better if they are done with enough time for Fido to be back to normal before the trip.

- Let your veterinarian know where Fido will be staying before your trip, even if a different veterinarian is used during an emergency yours should be contacted by the emergency veterinarian caring for your dog.

- Fill out all paper work; ensure that food, toys, blanket, medications, supplements are well marked with Fido's name.

- Know any health requirements; again if vaccinations or flea treatments are required it's best to administrator a week or two before your trip.

At Home and On The Drive

- Pack your luggage and your dog supplies when Fido is NOT around. If possible a few days or even the week before. You can add the last minute things the day of.

- Double check all document forms, food, toys, bedding, medications and supplements before heading out. Then triple check for all medications.

- Consider bringing jackets for short haired dogs if the weather is questionable.

- Make sure to have something with home smells to connect Fido with the family like an unwashed blanket, bed, toys or a towel that you kept in your bed for a night or two.

- Don't give extra amounts of food on check-in day. This can cause indigestion or other issues. For some dogs it's best to postpone feeding before heading out.

- Don't overcompensate the days before your trip; you may want to spend a little less time with Fido instead of more as it will help him when you are not around. But don't cut back on the walks and exercise; it's best if Fido can get a lot of activity before heading on vacation.

- If possible take Fido for a walk or hike before or on the way to the boarding facility, providing fun exercise with mom & dad will help the first few hours during their stay.

- If members of the family can't stay calm and upbeat during drop-off then leave them at home, only bring calm members.

- If Fido is a rescue dog, it's even more important that they know they are going to a fun place and you will be back to take them home again.

- If needed give yourself and Fido calming sprays like "Rescue Remedy" before you leave the home. Apply inside cars, crates, and bedding. (Aromatherapy and flower essences can be found at natural pet stores, whole food or other holistic health stores)

- Communicate to Fido where he is going, where you are going and that he and the humans are all safe and will be well taken care of and will be having fun. Just talk with full intention that he understands, use positive statements. Many think that dogs recognize positive energy even if they don't know the exact words.

- Drive Fido yourself if at all possible, shuttles and other services should only be used if he is used to them, this is most important for the first few trips.

- If you are lucky you may have a dog who takes it all in stride!

At The Pet Care Center or Dog Care Provider

- Review all medical, supplements, food, emotional or health considerations with the caregivers before you leave.

- Be honest about any oddities or issues to help the caregivers care for Fido. Does he chew, bark, dig, climb or have digestive issues? Is he afraid of loud noise or thunder? Does he not like a specific breed of dog?

- Do not apologize to Fido, they will sense if you are upset and it will cause him to be upset himself.

- You can say good-bye if you are calm, in fact it's good to let him know how long you will be away and let him know you are safe and camp will be a fun place.

- If your dog is dominant or feels it's his job to protect the home then have the staff put him in his room or run, this will reduce any confusion on him thinking he needs to protect the space for mom or dad.

- When dropping off Fido stay cool and try not to get emotional, if you are stressed out at the pickup and drop-off it may upset your pup. He may pick up on your sadness or nervousness.

- Fido should not see your car drive away, its' best for him not to know the direction that he could follow.

During The Trip

- Rest assured that Fido is doing well and having fun. Your peace of mind will connect with him.

- Do call and/or email occasionally if that will help you have a better trip.

- Ask if some photos or videos can be sent via email or phone of Fido playing or enjoying himself.

- Be cautious of having media sent to services like facebook wall as everyone will know you are away from home.

- Know that if you don't hear anything then assume that all is well as you know they have your contact information. . . no news is good news ☺.

Picking up

- When you come back from your trip, if possible unpack and get the house organized with family smells before bringing Fido home, this will help him to know all is well.

- When picking up, stay calm to show Fido that life is normal; this will help now and for future stays.

- When you pick up Fido he should be calm and either happy to see you or just overall happy/content. If he is depressed determine if the place is a good match for your pup.

- Ask how Fido did during the stay. Any problems with eating, drinking, diarrhea or other tummy issues? Did he show any signs of separation anxiety? Did he play well with the other dogs? Any aggression with humans? How about bedding or toys, did he tear any up? Any suggestions to help him at home or for next trips?

- Do look over your pup, if they played with other dogs they may have gotten dirty, a scrape or two and even picked up a flea. Review if this would be normal for the type of facility due to an active, group, country setting or if the caretakers may not be watching appropriately or the facility was unkempt.

Once Home

- Only provide small amounts of water and don't feed for at least 4 hours so that Fido is calm before eating. If he gulps lots of water or eats too quickly he could have tummy issues or diarrhea.

- On the way home and the first few days don't give special treats. Consider adding tummy support like canned pumpkin, enzyme's, and probiotic's to his normal food.

- A sign of a happy experience is when Fido comes home and acts like he was gone for just a few hours, he may be tired but overall his energy and mood is normal.

- Know your pup may be tired from the activity so he may sleep more the first few days at home.

- Contact the facility if there are any questions or concerns about behavior after coming home. If Fido is tired he is most likely tired from playing or the change of environment; but if you are concerned don't worry about calling or even checking with a veterinarian.

- Wait for any optional health procedures for a few weeks so Fido can be at his best.

- If you had a "great" experience let the owners know and post a review on Yelp, Angies List, Facebook, Google Plus and other sites. Share marketing material with coworkers, vets, dog trainers and pet stores.

- If you had a bad experience first contact the facility owner or manager to review what happened and if there is a justifiable explanation. If your dog has physical distress, take them to a vet for an evaluation.

- If you do not receive adequate results post your experience on web sites like Yelp, Angies List, Facebook and the Better Business Bureau. If the facility is a member of any certification then contact that agency.

Following these easy steps will help Fido and the whole family have a great boarding experience.

Chapter 7
Final Thoughts

As the primary caregiver of our furry friends we sometimes don't take enough time for ourselves. Having the ability to travel and experience new places, knowing you can be available to help family or travel for work helps support a well-adjusted life. Time away from our normal life enables us to have more energy for ourselves and all our family members, be they two legged or four legged. Reliable dog care you trust is an important factor in being a canine parent in today's world.

My wish is that Fido enjoys new experiences to build balance and confidence; whether exploring the back roads of America with Mom and Dad, playing with other guests at dog ranches or learning new things from in home care givers and trainers. The goal is to help Fido grow and to have a healthy mind and body and to be a happy dog.

Remember to trust your inner voice when reviewing caregivers, dog facilities or other animal care services. Check their references, read online review sites, visit the physical locations and most important go with your gut feeling. If you are not comfortable then you will not feel secure when you travel and this can translate to Fido.

If you are in the Seattle and Puget Sound area we would love to show you Mystic Mountain Pet Retreat in Monroe, Washington or our sister facility, Mountain View Dog Ranch in Snohomish, Washington.

Please visit our web site for additional information to help you and your animal friends to have a more balanced and safe life together. www.YourPetAdvocate.com

Some of the checklists and forms you will find are:

- Bring Fido with you on your travels.

- In your own home or care of Fido at another home.

- List of items to bring or have for Fido.

- Research steps on how to find caregivers.

- What to ask during initial communications with a professional or non-professional caregiver.

- Checklist for when you visit a professional dog care facility and what to look for.

- Forms that includes health issues, history, veterinarian spending and special needs.

- Forms with all your contacts: veterinarians, backup caregivers, friends, your trip info and instructions.

I hope you enjoyed reading this book as much as I enjoyed writing it. My wish is that you will find great care for Fido so you can enjoy traveling and seeing the world or just visiting family in other towns.

Cindy J Hill
Your Pet Advocate

"Helping you choose the best animal care for your family"

Free Check Lists at www.YourPetAdvocate.com

Acknowledgments

I wanted to thank everyone who helped with the completion of this book. A special thanks to Brad Hill for revising all my photos to the new format; Rebecca Klingler, Jody Pomper and Christine Young for listening to my ideas and many hours of editing; Craig Duswalt for providing a great writing system to get my ideas on paper; and other friends and family who supported me on this venture. While the book is only about 100 pages the time involved seemed like it should be about 500 pages!

Research Notes

Free Check Lists at www.YourPetAdvocate.com

Research Notes

_____

_____

_____

_____

_____

_____

_____

_____

_____

_____

_____

_____

_____

_____

_____

_____

_____

_____

Research Notes

Free Check Lists at www.YourPetAdvocate.com

Research Notes

_____

_____

_____

_____

_____

_____

_____

_____

_____

_____

_____

_____

_____

_____

_____

_____

_____

Research Notes

Free Check Lists at www.YourPetAdvocate.com

Research Notes

_____

_____

_____

_____

_____

_____

_____

_____

_____

_____

_____

_____

_____

_____

_____

_____

Made in the USA
Charleston, SC
10 May 2012